A Parent's Guide for Journaling to Their Child

Simple Strategies for Writing Heartfelt
Love Letters to Your Child

A Parent's Guide for Journaling to Their Child

Simple Strategies for Writing Heartfelt
Love Letters to Your Child

RONI WING LAMBRECHT
In Loving Memory of Dalton John Lambrecht

Companion Guide to:
PARENTING
at Your BEST

A Parent's Guide for Journaling to Their Child:
Simple Strategies for Writing Heartfelt Love Letters to Your Child
Published by 3 Hearts Press, Castle Rock, CO

Copyright ©2017 Roni Wing Lambrecht. All rights reserved.

No part of this book may be reproduced or transmitted in any form or by any means, mechanical or electronic, including photocopying or recording, or by any information storage or retrieval system, or transmitted by email without permission in writing from the publisher/author, except by a reviewer who may quote passages in a review.

ISBN: 978-0-9979298-3-6

Wing Lambrecht, Roni, Author
A Parent's Guide for Journaling to Their Child:
Simple Strategies for Writing Heartfelt Love Letters to Your Child
Roni Wing Lambrecht

JOURNAL GUIDE

Cover Design: Roni Lambrecht and
Victoria Wolf of Red Wolf Publishing
Cover Photos of Glamis Sand Dunes and Journal by Roni Lambrecht
Author's Photo: Britt Nemeth Photography
Book Design & Layout: Roni Lambrecht and Andrea Costantine
Publishing Consultant: Polly Letofsky of My Word Publishing

QUANTITY PURCHASES:
Schools, companies, professional groups, clubs, and other organizations may qualify for special terms when ordering quantities of this title. For information, email DoitForDalton@gmail.com.

DISCLAIMER: Neither the author nor the publisher assumes any responsibility for errors, omissions, or contrary interpretations of the subject matter herein. Any perceived slight of any individual or organization is purely unintentional.

All rights reserved by Roni Wing Lambrecht and 3 Hearts Press
This book is printed in the United States of America.

Dear Parent, Guardian, Grandparent, Aunt, Uncle, or other Special Adult in a child's life:

Congratulations on taking the first step in writing to your child! It is an honor that you chose this guide to help you along your writing journey.

You may wonder why I took the time to develop a guide like this. You see, my husband and I lost our only child in a tragic accident in 2013. Since then, we've been very blessed to have many people who have wanted to help us in our grieving process. So, when people ask what they can do to help, we always ask them to write love letters to their own children, grandchildren, nieces, nephews, or other loved ones as often as possible. We also ask them to teach their children how to write love letters to them in return. There have been a large number of people who have said they'd love to do so, but they didn't have any idea where to start. And so the idea of this journal guide was born...

We know that many people have difficulties knowing where to begin writing or what to write about, so, on the following pages, we've given you several writing topics which can help you be successful in writing to the important children in your life. The topics are separated into sections: Past, Present, and Future, as each one can touch your heart at any given time. Think about things you'd want them to know, if you weren't here to tell them. Be honest and forthcoming. Write about it all, knowing any written words from you are priceless to your child, whether they are still children or grown adults.

Your next step is to purchase a journal that "speaks to you," as they say; one that is beautiful to you, one that you wish to give to your child some day in the future, one to last a lifetime, or many lifetimes...

With Simple Strategies for Writing Heartfelt Love Letters to Your Child

With love and best wishes for a long,
happy life with your babies,
their babies, and beyond,

Dalton's Parents,
Roni & John Lambrecht

General Tips & Reminders

- ♥ Include the date and location on each of your writings.
- ♥ Write in first person using me, myself, I, you, we, us, etc.
- ♥ Write with detail and clarity so, when your child has the opportunity to read this journal in the future, they can sense everything about the moment you were writing to them.
- ♥ Think of the five senses: sight, smell, sound, taste, and touch. Use them every time you write.

- ♥ You could include great quotes, poetry, or song lyrics that have special significance to you with each journal entry.
- ♥ Paste special treasures you found on entries where you write about special "field trips" with your child (tree leaves, flowers, menus, movies, ticket stubs, amusement parks, zoos, museums, airline tickets, pictures you colored together, etc.)

Past
Where Did Your Child Come From?
All About You...

Your Family

- ♥ What were the names and birthdates of your family members: parents, siblings, grandparents, pets, etc. (Think of a family tree.)
- ♥ Write about your parents, your child's grandparents, in great detail, using your five senses. Which one are you most like/most relate to? Why?
- ♥ In regards to your parents (the child's grandparents), what did you learn about

parenting from them that you wish to continue with your child? What will you do differently? Why?
♥ Describe any special family heirlooms you wish to hand down to your children.

Your Childhood

♥ What was the name of each school you attended? Did you graduate? Did you go to college? Did you receive a degree? If so, share the details.
♥ What was your favorite activity as a child?
♥ Do you remember your favorite childhood toy? Describe and add a photo or drawing of it.
♥ What was your "safe place" as a child?
♥ What do you remember most about specific ages as a child? (kindergarten, elementary, middle school, junior high, high school, Sweet 16, first kiss, first boyfriend/girlfriend, etc.).
♥ Who were your best friends growing up?

Describe them in detail from their names to the way they looked and acted. Do you still talk to them or see them?
- ♥ What were some of the memories you have of each friend? What did you do for fun?
- ♥ Did you participate in a daily/weekly activity as a child that has had a lifelong impact? Explain.
- ♥ Are there activities that you did not participate in as a child that you wish you had?

Becoming An Adult

- ♥ Write about the birth of your child. Typical details should be included like name, date, time, place, height, weight, length, etc. You might explain the trials and tribulations of pregnancy. Who was there to share the special day. Who was the OBGYN? Was the birth recorded on video? If so, where is the video located? Did people come help in the days and weeks following the birth? Who and how did they help? Where did your child's name derive from? Best gifts received and from who? If you already have these things notated in a baby book, be sure to note somewhere in this journal where that baby book is located.

♥ Get a newspaper (including ads) from the day your child was born and keep it in a safe place. Tell them about the details of that day in this journal and where the newspaper is located. Write about the costs of certain things like milk, a dozen eggs, fuel. Write about the top songs, artists, book and movie releases.

♥ What did you imagine life would be like as a grown up before it happened? What's reality like as an adult? What are the best and worst parts of being an adult?

♥ How did you meet and fall in love with your spouse/partner?

♥ Explain the moment you knew your spouse/partner was "the one" for you.

♥ What do you love most about your

- spouse/partner?
- ♥ Describe how you feel about religion, faith, and spirituality? Do you practice one regularly? Why did you choose it? Does it bring you peace?
- ♥ List a few words you would use to describe yourself.
- ♥ What are you doing to make the world a better place?
- ♥ Are there big events or circumstances in your life that made you who you are? What are they and why do you think they had such a big impact on you? (Think about awards and achievements, most happy, sad, or embarrassing moments, births, deaths, accidents, moments that made world history, etc.)
- ♥ What are you proud of about yourself?
- ♥ What would you change about yourself? Why?
- ♥ What were some of the things invented during your lifetime? (Microwaves, Cell Phones, Internet, FaceBook, etc.)
- ♥ When did you get your first cell phone?

Why?
- When did you join the internet/email/social media world, if at all? Why?
- What do you consider your greatest blessings? Why?
- What's the best advice you ever received? From whom? Why is it the best?
- If you could have the perfect day - no limits - who would you be with and what would you do?
- What is your best quality?
- What is your biggest weakness/fear?
- If there was one event you could change in your life, what would it be and why?
- If there was one event in history that did not directly affect you that you could change, what event would that be and why?
- Do you have any bad habits? What are they? Have you ever tried to stop them?
- What are your best habits? How did you make them work for you?
- Is your health important to you? Explain why or why not.

- ♥ What makes you feel the most loved?
- ♥ What/where is your "safe" place?
- ♥ Do you own something that has extreme value to you, but no value to anyone else? Describe it in detail: where you got it, what it is, etc. Why is it of so much value to you?
- ♥ Do you have any tattoos? If so, where are they and what is their significance?
- ♥ What's on your bucket list? Is there anything your child could help you fulfill?
- ♥ Write about the people you admire or look up to and why.
- ♥ Who has been a mentor to you? How? For what purpose? What have you done to thank them for their mentorship?
- ♥ Have you been a mentor to someone else? How? For what purpose? How did it make you feel to help someone else?
- ♥ Are there any decisions you've made in your life that you wish you could change? Why?
- ♥ Who do you count on to help you through

the tough times?
- ♥ What do you believe are good financial investments today? If you had extra money today, what would you invest in?
- ♥ What are your favorites and why?
  - ♥ Artist
  - ♥ Author
  - ♥ Band/Performer
  - ♥ Birthday Celebration
  - ♥ Book/Book Series
  - ♥ Chore
  - ♥ Class/Subject
  - ♥ Clothing: outfit, shirt, pants, jeans, socks, hat, coat, etc.
  - ♥ Color
  - ♥ Dance
  - ♥ Dessert
  - ♥ Drink
  - ♥ Food (What food do you refuse to eat – why?)
  - ♥ Game/Puzzle
  - ♥ Hobby
  - ♥ Holiday
  - ♥ Movie/Movie Series

- ♥ Number
- ♥ People: family, friends, teachers, neighbors, etc.
- ♥ Place
- ♥ Recipe
- ♥ Restaurant
- ♥ Season: Spring, Summer, Fall, Winter
- ♥ Song
- ♥ Sport
- ♥ Team
- ♥ Television Show/Series

Death

- ♥ What do you believe happens when we die? Where do we go? What do we do? Do you believe life is pre-destined/already written? Describe your idea of what happens upon death in detail.
- ♥ How do you feel about assisted suicide in certain circumstances?
- ♥ When you die, what do you hope your family and friends remember most?
- ♥ What would you like included in your eulogy?

Present

Child

- ♥ How does your child look today? Be descriptive using eye and hair color, height, weight. Compare the size of their hands and feet to something you will always have handy. What are they wearing? Take a photo and paste it in the journal.
- ♥ List a few words you would use to describe your child.
- ♥ What makes you most proud to be your

childs' parent?
- ♥ Write about your child like they are the top news story of the day for the whole world to see on TV.
- ♥ Does your child have a favorite blanket or stuffed animal or something else that they must have with them all the time, wherever they go? If so, describe it in detail using all 5 senses. Take a photo of your child with that item and paste on the left page of your description.
- ♥ Did something big or funny happen today with your child? Tell the story in detail so that you can go there again every time you read about it.
- ♥ What are your daily schedules like from the time you get up to the time you go to bed? (Describe the last week in detail.)
- ♥ What do you typically say and do when saying goodbye to each other for the day (before school/work)?
- ♥ Do you have any specific rituals - a common saying, a big hug, after school, bedtime, weekends, etc?

With Simple Strategies for Writing Heartfelt Love Letters to Your Child

- ♥ Ask your child to draw a picture of your family/home and explain it to you. Paste the picture in the journal. If they aren't old enough to write yet, write what they told you in the journal. Ask them to do this annually and see how it progresses.
- ♥ Trace your hand on a sheet of paper and then ask your child to trace their hand within yours. Paste the picture in the journal. Do this annually and see how much they grow!
- ♥ Describe your child's laughter and how it makes you feel.
- ♥ Describe your child's personality in detail.
- ♥ What music do you listen to or sing with your child? When do you listen/sing with them?
- ♥ What's the most recent television show or movie you watched together? How did your child react?
- ♥ Describe a typical trip to the store with your child.
- ♥ What does your child like to do on a lazy

day around home?
- ♥ What are your child's "tells?" (How do you know if they're fibbing, don't like something, if they are truly happy, etc.?)
- ♥ How does your child do in school academically and socially?
- ♥ Does your child take charge or do they typically follow the leader? Describe an example of this?
- ♥ Describe your child's manners; what they do well and what they need to work on.
- ♥ What soothes your child when they are upset?
- ♥ Where is your child's "safe place?"
- ♥ What does your child look forward to?
- ♥ Is your child saving their money for something special? How do you think they'll feel when they achieve their goal of buying it? Or, have they already done this for the first time? How did it end up?
- ♥ What is your child studying in school? Are there things they are not being taught that you wish they were? Is there something they are being taught you

wish they were not being taught?
- ♥ Who are your child's closest friends (include first and last names)? Are they siblings, cousins, neighbors, school friends?
- ♥ What is something your child does that drives you crazy?
- ♥ Has your child been disappointed somehow? What happened? How did you help them through the experience?
- ♥ Does your child have any habits; good or bad?
- ♥ What is your child selfish about?
- ♥ In what ways is your child the most giving?
- ♥ What chores is your child responsible for? Which chores do they like/dislike the most?
- ♥ Has your child made a mistake that caused strife at home/school? How did you help them through the experience and show them how to take responsibility for their actions?
- ♥ Who does your child look up to or want

to be like? Why?
- ♥ What does your child want to do when they grow up? Why?
- ♥ If you could give your child one specific line of advice, what would it be and why?
- ♥ What fears does your child have? How will you help them to grow out of them?
- ♥ Does your child have any recurring dreams or nightmares? Explain them here just as they explain them to you. What is their state of mind? Does the dream/nightmare excite, scare, upset them? How do you calm them?
- ♥ What do you see in your child that they cannot see in themselves?
- ♥ What would you change about your child, if you could? Why?
- ♥ What are some of the things that have been invented/discovered in your child's lifetime?
- ♥ Is there something you feel like your child understands better than you do? Why?
- ♥ Are there any decisions you've made

for your child that you wish you could change? Why?

♥ Schedule a movie date with your child to watch your favorite movie from when you grew up. Describe their reaction and what they thought of the movie.

♥ What are the qualities you wish your child would look for and find in friends or their future spouse?

♥ Words that have altered your vocabulary...
  ♥ While it's important to correct our children when they use the wrong vocabulary, it's also good to make it fun when we're correcting them. When these moments happen, write the words they used and also their real meanings.
  ♥ Keep track of words or phrases that are new during their lifetime. (Words like "cell phone," "texting," "Twitter," and "Facebook," are all new since I was born.)

♥ Using magazines or newspapers, cut out words that stand out to you when you

think of your child and paste them in a random pattern in this journal.
- ♥ List the different titles/descriptions you and your child have and their importance:
  - ♥ Do this with your child annually and see how their priorities change over time.
  - ♥ Parent examples: mother/father, spouse/partner, daughter/son, granddaughter/grandson, sister/brother, niece/nephew, cousin, friend, neighbor, volunteer, employee, business owner, student, etc.
  - ♥ Child examples: daughter/son, granddaughter/grandson, sister/brother, niece/nephew, cousin, friend, neighbor, volunteer, employee, business owner, student, etc.
  - ♥ This is a great way to prioritize when it feels like things at home are out-of-order.
- ♥ Favorites - for these, you'll ask your child what their favorites are. It's also fun to find out why they have chosen these as

their favorites. You might also ask about their dislikes.

- ♥ Artist
- ♥ Author
- ♥ Band/Performer
- ♥ Birthday Celebration
- ♥ Book/Book Series
- ♥ Chore
- ♥ Class/Subject
- ♥ Clothing: outfit, shirt, pants, jeans, socks, hat, coat, etc.
- ♥ Color
- ♥ Dance
- ♥ Dessert
- ♥ Drink
- ♥ Food (What food do they refuse to eat - why?)
- ♥ Game/Puzzle
- ♥ Hobby
- ♥ Holiday
- ♥ Movie/Movie Series
- ♥ Number
- ♥ People: family, friends, teachers, neighbors, etc.

- ♥ Place
- ♥ Recipe
- ♥ Restaurant
- ♥ Season: Spring, Summer, Fall, Winter
- ♥ Song
- ♥ Sport
- ♥ Team
- ♥ Television Show/Series

Home/Family

- ♥ Where do you live? What is your exact address? What's the neighborhood called? Explain in vivid detail as if it's the first time you are walking onto your property and into your home.
- ♥ Why do you live here; in this house, this city, this state?
- ♥ Who lives with you (include first and last names if not immediate family)?
- ♥ Do you have pets? If so, describe them in detail. What are their names?
- ♥ What are your favorite places to visit as a family? Explain in vivid detail. How

much does it cost to go there? How long do you typically stay? What's the best part of going there?
- ♥ What are your favorite family activities?
- ♥ Discuss your family traditions in detail including those of your spouse/partner's family.
- ♥ Describe a special holiday or event in your household using all five senses and the joy it creates to watch your child enjoy it.
- ♥ Open your refrigerator and pantry. Describe what's inside each.
- ♥ List some of the items you purchase on a regular basis and their costs (milk, eggs, cereal, toilet paper, fuel, insurance, etc.). You could also paste receipts for those items in the journal.

Future Topics

- ♥ Of your previous experiences in life, what do you hope your child does just like you? Why?
- ♥ Of your previous experiences in life, what do you hope your child avoids completely? Why?
- ♥ If you could choose three characteristics your child learns from you, what would they be? Why?
- ♥ If you could choose three characteristics your child learns from their other parent, what would they be? Why?

- ♥ What are your goals and aspirations for your child? Why?
- ♥ What are your child's goals for themselves? Discuss this in detail with them annually.
- ♥ Where do you hope to take your child on vacation?
- ♥ Where do you hope your child will be able to travel in their lifetime?
- ♥ If you could write your child's resume for them, what would you say to an employer?
- ♥ What characteristics do you hope your child finds in their future mate? Why? Are there specific traits that you believe their mate should have to balance your child?
- ♥ If something were to happen to you, who do you hope will take care of your child? Why? Be specific.

An excerpt from the author's
award-winning book:

PARENTING at Your BEST

Powerful Reflections and Straightforward Tips
for Becoming a Mindful Parent

Available at Amazon.com

Write Your Way Into My Heart

I am a firm believer that anyone can say anything, but it doesn't hold much worth until it's in writing, and so I begin with *Dalton's Journal;* one of the most important accomplishments of my life...

When I was pregnant, I began writing a journal to our baby. I started with how proud I was to be its mommy, how much I adored John, and how John was going to make such a great daddy. I told the baby about our lives, how we met and fell in love, what we hoped we could teach him/her, and how scared and excited we were to be parents.

While I didn't write in it as often as I should have, I wrote about a lot of things, like how tired I was, and what a struggle it was to raise a headstrong kid. I wrote about his laugh and his friends and school and teachers. More often than not, I would write funny stories about things Dalton said or things that had happened; things I would never want to forget (the stories that make you laugh out loud years later when you read them). As a parent, there are so many breathtaking memories that often get pushed aside because the daily minutia takes up so much of our brains. There are stories in that journal I wanted to remember forever when I wrote them down, and there are many

> It has reminded us over and over what a full life we had with our angel and the strength of our love for one another.

that I had completely forgotten until I read them again after Dalton passed away.

When Dalton was about 8 or 9, he asked me what I was writing, and I told him I had been writing him a long love letter since before he was born. He wanted to read it *right then and there*. We even wrestled for it, but I won. I told him that he had to wait until his 18th birthday, and that, even then, it always had to "live" at my house so I could keep reading it too.

Since the accident, so much is a blur, yet there is no question in our minds that *Dalton's Journal* saved our marriage, and it has saved us so many times between then and now. It has reminded us over and over what a full life we had with our angel and the strength of our love for one another. This is how it happened...

My parents flew out to be with us after Dalton passed away and I hadn't been outside the camper, nor had I showered or eaten. My mom forced me into the shower and then dressed me. She made John do the same thing. Then she told us we had to go for a walk and get some fresh air. For some reason, I grabbed

Dalton's Journal on the way out the door. After a while, we came to a beautiful sitting area where I sat down and opened it. I began reading and crying. John asked me if I would read it to him and I said, "No. This was for Dalton." John begged me, and so I began reading to him. The first several pages were written before Dalton was ever born. I had written all about John and I, how we fell in love, and how much we were looking forward to meeting our baby. I had also written how lucky the baby would be to have John as its daddy, how much I adored John, and how lucky I was to call him my husband and my best friend.

After I read several pages, John said, "I never knew you felt that way." I couldn't believe my ears! After all the years of cards and poems I had written him and the countless times I had told him directly how much I loved him, how did he not know this?!?! What?!?!

He said, "I never heard you tell anyone else that before." It was then and there, after nearly 20 years of marriage, that I felt like we completely understood each other. I believe Dalton had a hand in making me pick up his journal and read to John. The statistics of parents divorcing after they've lost their only child are staggering, and we're very blessed to still be together.

Straightforward Tips for Parenting at Your Best

I've always been a proponent of journaling and writing love letters to our kids (and requiring them to learn how to write back). Because of this, I have always given journals as baby gifts. In fact, my second and third books, *A Parents Guide for Journaling to Their Child* and *A Parent's Journal to Their Child* (available now!!!), are actually a guide and a parenting journal with advice and prompts to help parents everywhere write ongoing love letters to their kids.

So, please, if you don't do anything else, please do this...

> Write love letters to your child.

Journal of Love Letters for Each Child

Get a journal for each of your kids and start writing in it. Take it from parents who know the value of great memories... Write your child love letters and share stories about funny things they say or do, how they look, and what they like to wear. Include funny reactions they have, daily routines, traditions, the music they love to listen to, songs you like to sing together, hobbies, habits, family, friends, teachers, neighbors, daily schedules, etc. Share stories about your love for your spouse/partner, how you met and fell in love. Share times you laugh and cry and struggle to keep your sanity because your child is driving you crazy. Share your personal goals and dreams, as well as those you wish for them. Be honest and forthcoming. Write about it all. This doesn't have to be a daily task, but it's important to write several times a year at the very least. So much happens that could easily be forgotten if it wasn't written down. I also made it a priority to write to Dalton anytime something really funny or "big" happened.

Other great writing endeavors; all of which will take some guidance from you to your kids...

Thankful Journal

Start a Thankful Journal that you each write in every night before bed. All three of us had matching notebooks, and the process was as follows. Every night before bed, we sat on Dalton's bed and wrote in our Thankful Journals:
- ♥ Today, I am thankful for...
- ♥ Five good things about today were...
- ♥ Something I like about myself is...

For us, this only lasted a few months, but it was a good training tool to get us to talk about things more often and with more clarity. I wish I could say this was my idea, but if I remember correctly, this idea came from an Oprah show.

Story Journal

We have a good friend that told us about this one that she does with her grandkids.

- ♥ Writer 1: Writes the beginning of a story (1-2 pages), then gives the journal to Writer 2.
- ♥ Writer 2: Reads Writer 1's story and writes the ending (1-2 pages), then turns the page and starts a completely new story (1-2 pages), then gives the journal to Writer 1.
- ♥ Writer 1: Reads the entire story that they wrote together and gives it a title, then reads Writer 2's new story and writes the ending (1-2 pages), then turns the page and starts a completely new story (1-2 pages), then gives the journal to Writer 2.
- ♥ Writer 2: Reads the entire story that they wrote together and gives it a title, then reads Writer 1's new story and writes the ending (1-2 pages), then turns the

page and starts a completely new story (1-2 pages), then gives the journal to Writer 1.

You can come up with your own idea of how to do it, but the idea is that the stories go back and forth and, as the kids grow, you will clearly see how their writing and imagination improves.

Appreciation Journal

I've seen this done with parents and kids, grandparents and grandchildren, between bosses and co-workers, and between teachers and students. The idea is to write something nice about someone and give it to them. It could be as simple as telling your child you think they did a great job in an activity or thanking them for helping out without being asked. Then you give it to them, and later they'll return it to you thanking you just for being you or doing something nice for them. These are great for kids who have a hard time expressing their feelings face to face, and they help everyone appreciate the good in life, versus dwelling on the bad.

Vacation Journals

Before each family vacation or camping trip, get a small notebook and have your children write in it each day or night of the trip to explain what they did, who they were with, what they enjoyed and what they didn't, food they ate, etc. They can also draw pictures of the daily events. Not only will you be able to see how their writing/drawing progresses over the years, but you will also be helping them learn how to express themselves and improve their writing. It can also be very helpful years later if you ever have questions about where or when a photo was taken, what you did while you were there, or who was on the trip with you.

Birthday Envelopes

This is a great idea I found on social media...
    Every year, on their birthday, write a letter

to your child (grandchild, niece, nephew, neighbor, etc.) and add a small amount of cash to the envelope with the letter. Do this each year and give all the envelopes to your child for graduation. They'll get 17 or 18 years of letters, a good amount of cash, and they'll have a graduation present that lasts a lifetime.

Birthday, Greeting, and Thank You Cards

I have always been a stickler about writing nice cards. Dalton learned from an early age that before special days for others, he was expected to write a nice card to them. He also knew that after every birthday and Christmas, he'd be spending at least an hour writing personalized thank-you cards for the gifts he received and places he got to go. He loathed it at first, but then found it to be fun and started writing poetry and goofy stories in his cards to tell people what he used his gift for. My parents actually have all of the cards Dalton gave them hanging on their wall, including the one where he wrote, *"It's a pleasure being your grandson."* (That was one we all thought was pretty cute!) Additionally, I always explained to Dalton the importance of appreciating and validating someone and making sure to write something special in each card he wrote so that his words *mattered* and they were *worth reading.* Not to mention, I thought it was important that I raise a young man who knows how to write a love letter to his own wife and children in the future.

When Dalton was 14, he wrote me this amazing birthday card...

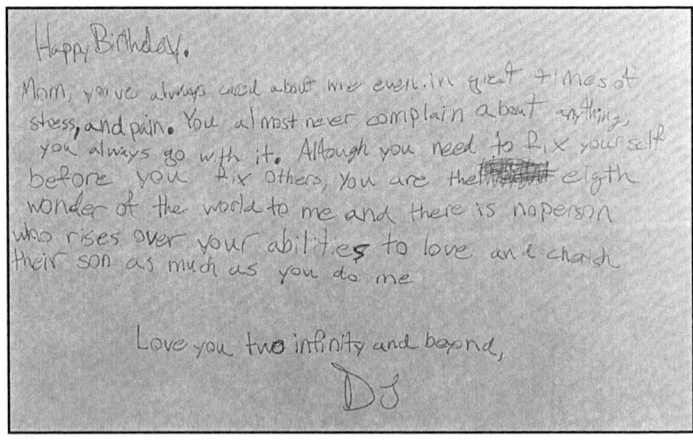

Since receiving this card, it has been my most prized possession. I am so blessed to have had a child who used his talents and teachings to write down his love for me so plainly. Someday soon, it will be tattooed on my right arm.

To teach your children, grandchildren, nieces, nephews, and friends this valuable lesson, try this...

1. Make sure you lead by example by writing them nice cards.
2. Along with their gifts for each birthday and holiday, give each child a box of thank you cards and stamps so they have them handy after the holiday. They might just surprise you!

I do hope you enjoy writing to your child!

If this guide has helped you in any way, please share it with someone else.
It makes a great gift for weddings, baby showers, birthdays, and just because!
Thank you for sharing.

We welcome your comments and suggestions for additional guide questions and topics for future versions of this book. Please email DoItForDalton@gmail.com and put *"Guide"* in the subject line.

We also welcome your reviews.
Please post them on Amazon.com.

For speaking engagements or book club visits, please email
DoItForDalton@gmail.com.

Additional parenting resources can be found at www.DaltonsJournal.com

Author Bio

Known as a serial entrepreneur by her family and friends, Roni Wing Lambrecht has always been a forward thinker, spending her time working on projects to make life easier and more organized for everyone she connects with. Roni has run her own mortgage document preparation and closing company since 1996 and has been a REALTOR® since 2008.

Roni and her husband, John, have been married since 1995. Their beautiful son, Dalton, was with them for 15 years and left for Heaven just after Christmas 2013 due to injuries from an ATV accident. Dalton lived his short life creating smiles, laughter, and happiness by sharing his kind spirit and helping others through tough times. Roni and John continue his legacy by counting their blessings for the short time they had him and practicing random acts of kindness in his memory each and every day.

Roni and John live in Castle Rock, Colorado with their dog, Daxton. They spend most of their time remodeling and selling homes for their clients. Any free time is spent with their families in Colorado and Texas, and riding ATVs and camping in sand dunes across the U.S.

Roni's books, *Parenting At Your Best*, *A Parent's Journal to Their Child,* and *A Parent's Guide for Journaling to Their Child* are a tribute to Dalton, with anticipation that the stories and advice they offer will inspire others to excellence in their parenting.

Notes

Notes

Notes

Notes

#　Notes

Notes

Notes